WILLIAM SHA

Stratford-upon-Avon, 1578. A boy is sitting at a schooldesk. He listens to the teacher, reads his books, learns his lessons. What is he thinking about?

London, 1587. A young man is riding into London for the first time. He listens to the noise of the crowded streets, sees the great walls of the Tower of London, looks down at the waters of the River Thames. 'Sweet Thames, run softly, till I end my song.'

London, 1601. The boatmen on the River Thames are shouting to the crowds: 'Hurry, hurry, hurry! The Globe theatre is filling fast!' Two thousand people are crossing the river to see the latest play – *Hamlet*, by William Shakespeare.

This story about Shakespeare's life is told by his friend Toby. Toby is not a real person – perhaps Shakespeare had a friend like that, but we don't know. But all the other characters in the story were real people, who knew Will Shakespeare as a friend, actor, poet, and playwright. 'Gentle Shakespeare,' they called him, and they knew he was the greatest poet in England. His friend Ben Jonson wrote of him:

'He was not of an age, but for all time.'

OXFORD BOOKWORMS LIBRARY

True Stories

William Shakespeare

Stage 2 (700 headwords)

Series Editor: Jennifer Bassett
Founder Editor: Tricia Hedge
Activities Editors: Jennifer Bassett and Alison Baxter

For my father

JENNIFER BASSETT

The Life and Times of William Shakespeare

OXFORD UNIVERSITY PRESS

OXFORD
UNIVERSITY PRESS

Great Clarendon Street, Oxford OX2 6DP

Oxford University Press is a department of the University of Oxford.
It furthers the University's objective of excellence in research, scholarship,
and education by publishing worldwide in

Oxford New York

Auckland Cape Town Dar es Salaam Hong Kong Karachi
Kuala Lumpur Madrid Melbourne Mexico City Nairobi
New Delhi Shanghai Taipei Toronto

With offices in

Argentina Austria Brazil Chile Czech Republic France Greece
Guatemala Hungary Italy Japan Poland Portugal Singapore
South Korea Switzerland Thailand Turkey Ukraine Vietnam

OXFORD and OXFORD ENGLISH are registered trade marks of
Oxford University Press in the UK and in certain other countries

First published in Oxford Bookworms 1993

10 12 14 16 17 15 13 11

ISBN 978 0 19 479076 5

A complete recording of this Bookworms edition of
William Shakespeare is available on audio CD ISBN 978 0 19 479038 3

Printed in China

ACKNOWLEDGEMENTS

Original illustrations by: Richard Allen

*The publishers would like to thank the following
for their permission to reproduce illustrations:*
The British Library pp 17, 23, 30; The British Museum pp 10/11;
Dulwich Picture Gallery p 36; Robert Harding Picture Library pp 15, 28;
The International Shakespeare Globe Centre p 60;
National Portrait Gallery pp 26, 35, 40, 48; The Shakespeare Birthplace Trust,
by courtesy of the Records Office p 3; Shakespeare Centre Library,
Stratford-upon-Avon p 21

Word count (main text): 9135 words

For more information on the Oxford Bookworms Library,
visit www.oup.com/elt/gradedreaders

CONTENTS

1

Toby remembers

My name is Toby. I'm an old man, eighty-three this spring. My house is right in the middle of Stratford-upon-Avon, and I can watch the street market from my window. But I live very quietly now. I'm just an old man, sitting in a chair.

I once knew the greatest man in England. For thirty years I was his friend. I worked with him in the theatre, through the good times and the bad times. He was a good friend to me. He was also the best playwright, the best poet, that ever lived in England. Will Shakespeare was his name.

I saw all his plays in the theatre. People loved them. They shouted, laughed and cried, ate oranges, and called for more. All kinds of people. Kings, Queens, Princes, great lords and ladies, poor people, the boys who held the horses . . . everyone. Will Shakespeare could please them all.

All kinds of people . . . Will Shakespeare could please them all

He put me in a play once. Well, he used my name – Toby. *Twelfth Night* was the play, I remember. Sir Toby Belch. He was a big fat man, who liked drinking too much and having a good time. Queen Elizabeth the First watched that play – on Twelfth Night, the 6th of January, 1601. She liked it, too.

Will's dead now, of course. He's been dead more than thirty years, and no one sees his plays now. The Puritans have closed all the theatres. There's no singing, no dancing, no plays. It wasn't like that in my young days. We had a good time in London, Will and I . . .

I've no teeth now, and my hair has all fallen out, but I can still think – and remember. I remember when Will and I were young, just boys really . . .

2
Stratford-upon-Avon

It was a sunny day in October 1579 when I first met Will, just outside Stratford, near a big field of apple trees. I saw a boy up in one of the trees. He had red hair and looked about two years older than me.

'What are you doing up there?' I called.

'Just getting a few apples,' he said, smiling.

'Those are Farmer Nash's apples,' I said, 'and he'll send his dogs after you if he sees you.'

'Mr Nash has gone to market,' the boy said. 'Come on! They're good apples.'

The next minute I was up the tree with him. But Will was

wrong. Farmer Nash wasn't at the market, and a few minutes later we saw his angry red face above the wall on the far side of the field.

Will and I ran like the wind and only stopped when we reached the river. We sat down to eat our apples.

Will was fifteen, and lived in Henley Street, he told me. His father was John Shakespeare, and he had a sister, Joan, and two younger brothers, Gilbert and Richard. There was another sister who died, I learnt later. And the next year he had another brother, little Edmund – the baby of the family.

'Now, what about you?' he asked.

'There's only me and my sister,' I said. 'My parents are dead, and we live with my mother's brother. He's a shoe-maker in Ely Street and I work for him. What do you do?'

Shakespeare's home in Henley Street, Stratford

'I go to Mr Jenkins' school in Church Street,' Will said. 'Every day, from seven o'clock until five o'clock. Not Sundays, of course.'

I was sorry for him. 'Isn't it boring?' I asked.

'Sometimes. Usually it's all right.' He lay back and put his hands behind his head. 'But we have to read and learn all these

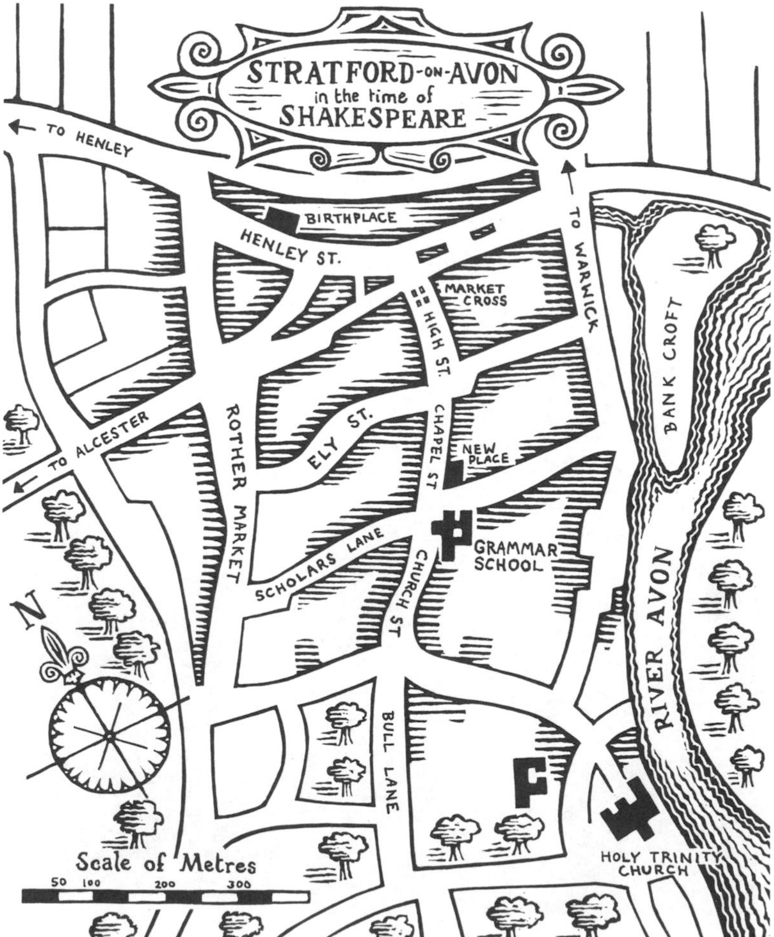

Latin writers. I want to read modern writers, and English writers, like Geoffrey Chaucer. Can *you* read?' he asked.

'Of course I can read!' I said. 'I went to school.'

Will sat up and began to eat another apple. 'I want to be a writer,' he said. 'A poet. I want that more than anything in the world.'

We were friends from that day, until the day he died. We met nearly every day, and he taught me a lot about books and poetry and writers. He always had his nose in a book.

When Will left school, he worked for his father in Henley Street. John Shakespeare was a glove-maker, and he had other business too, like buying and selling sheep. But Will wasn't interested.

'What are we going to do, Toby?' he said to me one day. 'We can't spend all our lives making shoes and gloves!'

Well,' I said, 'we could run away to sea and be sailors. Sail round the world, like Francis Drake.'

Drake sailed back to Plymouth in 1581, after his three-year journey round the world, but we were still in Stratford. We made lots of plans, but nothing ever came of them.

Will was still reading a lot and he was already writing poems himself. He sometimes showed them to me, and I said they were very good. I didn't really know anything about poetry then, but he was my friend.

Will was not happy with his writing. 'I've got so much to learn, Toby,' he said. 'So much to learn.'

Poor Will. He had a lot to learn about women, too. One day

in October 1582 he came to my house with a long face.

'I'll never leave Stratford,' he said.

'Why not?' I asked. 'We'll get away one day. You'll see.'

'Perhaps *you* will,' he said, 'but I'm going to be married in a few weeks' time. To Anne Hathaway.'

My mouth fell open and stayed open. 'Married! To Anne Hathaway? Is that the Hathaways over at Shottery?'

'Yes,' Will said. I was working on some shoes on the table, and Will picked one up and looked at it.

'Well, er, she's a fine girl, of course,' I said uncomfortably. 'But . . . but, Will, she's twenty-six and you're only eighteen!'

'I know,' Will said. 'But I've got to marry her.'

'Oh no!' I said. 'You mean, she's . . .'

'That's right,' said Will. 'In about six months' time I'm going to be a father.'

3

The actors come to town

Will married Anne Hathaway in November, and she came to live in Henley Street. John Shakespeare was pleased that his oldest son was married, but I don't think Will's mother wanted him to marry so young. Families cost a lot of money, and John Shakespeare was having a lot of money troubles in those days. Times were hard in Henley Street.

Susanna was born the next May. All babies look the same to me, but Will was very pleased with her.

'Look, Toby, she's got my eyes,' he said happily. 'She's

going to be as beautiful as the Queen of Egypt, and as clever as King Solomon.'

'Oh yes?' I said. 'All parents talk like that about their children. I don't believe a word of it.'

I didn't see much of Will's wife. I knew she didn't like me. To her, I was one of Will's wild friends, who got him into trouble. She came from a very serious, Puritan family. Lots of church-going, and no singing or dancing.

Soon there was another baby on the way, and one evening in February 1585 I hurried round to Henley Street to hear the news. Will's sister, Joan, opened the door, and then Will came running down the stairs.

'It's two of them!' he said. 'Twins! A girl and a boy. Isn't that wonderful!'

Will had some good friends, Hamnet and Judith Sadler, and he called the twins after them. John Shakespeare was very pleased to have his first grandson, and everyone was happy. For a while.

Will and I still went around together when we could. He was still reading, and writing, and soon I could see a change in him. He was twenty-three now, and he was not happy with his life.

'Stratford's too small, Toby,' he said. 'Too slow. Too quiet. Too boring. I've got to get away.'

'Yes, but how?' I asked. 'You've got a family – three young children, remember.'

He didn't answer.

In the summer months companies of players often came to small towns, and in 1587 five different companies came. Will and I always went to see the plays. Will loved to talk to the actors and to listen to all their stories of London.

The Queen's Men came to Stratford in June, and we went to see the play. I don't remember what it was. I know that I laughed a lot, and that Will said it was a stupid play, with not a word of poetry in it.

'Why don't you write a play yourself?' I told him.

'Write a play?' He laughed. 'Anne would never speak to me again.'

I didn't say anything, and Will looked at me and laughed again.

It happened a few months later. I walked into the

The Queen's Men came to Stratford in June.

Shakespeares' kitchen one evening, and there was Anne, with a red, angry face, shouting at the top of her voice.

'How can you do this to me? And what about the children—' Then she saw me and stopped.

Will was sitting at the table, and looked pleased to see me. 'I've told Anne,' he said quietly, 'that I'm going to live in London. I want to be an actor, and to write plays, if I can.'

'Plays!' screamed Anne. 'Acting! Actors are dirty, wicked people! They're all thieves and criminals! They drink all day and they never go to church—'

'Don't be stupid, Anne. You know that's not true. Listen. I'll come home when I can, but I must go to London. I can't do anything in Stratford.' He looked at me across the room. 'Are you coming with me, Toby?'

'How soon can we start?' I said.

4
A new life in London

It's two days' journey to London by horse, and Will talked all the way. His eyes were bright and excited. He was full of plans, and poems, and a love of life.

'I talked to one of the Queen's Men,' he told me. 'He said that he could find me work in the theatre. Acting, perhaps. Or helping to write some plays. I showed him some of my writing, and he was very interested.'

When we rode into London, I began to feel afraid. This was a big, big city, and we were just two unimportant young men from a small town. I'll never forget the noise, and the smells, and the crowds. There were 200,000 people living in the City of London – I never saw so many people before in my life.

We went down to the river Thames and saw the famous London Bridge, with all its shops and houses. Down the river was the Tower of London. Enemies of the Queen went into the Tower through the river gate, and mostly came out without their heads.

We found a small inn in Eastcheap, not too expensive, and had some bread, meat, and beer for our supper.

'Well, we're here!' Will said. 'At last!'

'Mmm,' I said. 'What do we do next?'

From Visscher's *View of London*

He laughed. 'Everything!'

The next day we began to look for work.

Those early years were wonderful. We didn't have much money, of course, and we had to work very hard. A new actor only got six shillings a week, and there wasn't work every week. I decided not to be an actor.

'Why not?' said Will. 'It's a great life.'

We were working that month for the Queen's Men at the theatre called The Curtain up in Shoreditch. Will was acting four small parts in two different plays. He played a soldier and

I'll never forget the noise, and the smells, and the crowds.

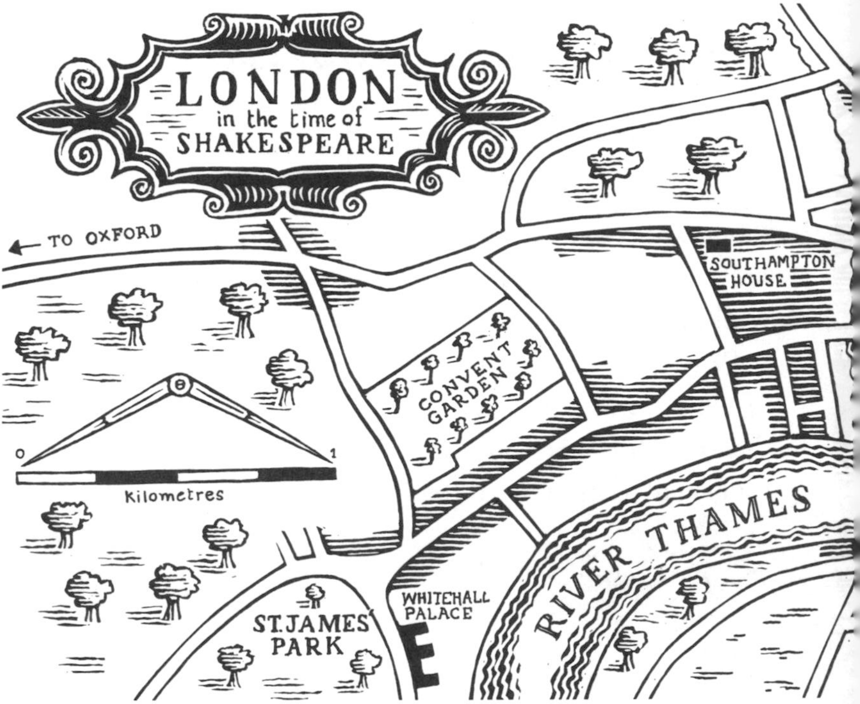

a murderer in one play, and in the other play he was a thief, and also an Italian lord in love with the Queen of the Night. And he loved it.

'I'm not clever like you,' I said. 'I can't remember all those words. I forget who I am! I say the soldier's words, when I'm an Italian lord. I come on stage too late, or too soon. I stand in all the wrong places . . .'

Will laughed. 'What are you going to do, then?'

'Costumes,' I said. 'And properties. I had a talk with John Heminges, and he said they need a new man to help with all the clothes and the other things.'

'Yes,' Will said slowly. 'You'll be good at that. Now, I've

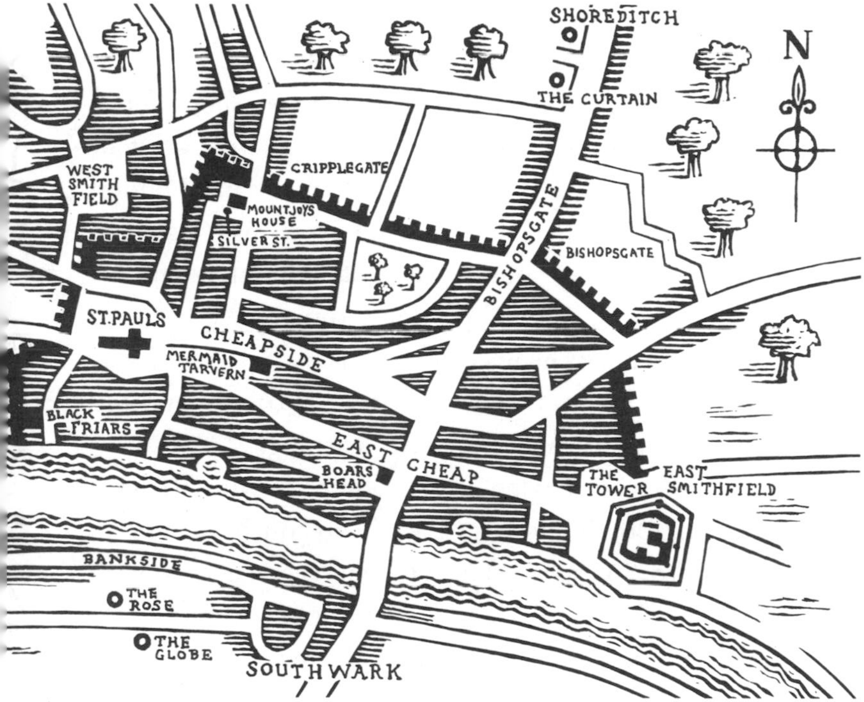

got a fight on stage tomorrow, and I have to die with lots of blood. How are you going to get me some blood?'

'I've already got it!' I smiled kindly at him. 'Sheep's blood. I got it down at Smithfield market this morning. You can have as much blood as you want. I'm keeping it warm for you!'

Will was good at acting. Not the best, but good. An actor had to do everything. He had to learn his words, of course – perhaps for six different plays at the same time. No theatre put on the same play every day. He had to dance, and sing, and play music. He had to jump, and fall, and fight. And the fights had to look real. The playgoers of London knew a real fight when they saw one.

John Heminges of the Queen's Men taught us both a lot. He was a good friend, then and for many years.

I had a lot to learn, too. I learnt how to make shoes out of brown paper. How to clean the actors' hats with a bit of bread. Then they looked like new again. I ran all over London to buy the best hair for the wigs. I learnt how to make fish, and fruit, and a piece of meat out of wood and coloured paper.

Will was busy day and night. I don't know when he slept. He was acting in plays, he was writing his own plays, he was reading books, he was meeting other writers, making friends . . . He was learning, learning, learning.

One day we were having a glass of beer with Richard Burbage at the Boar's Head in Eastcheap. Burbage was an actor with Lord Strange's Men. He was very friendly with Will.

'You've written four plays now, Will,' he said. 'They're good, and you're getting better all the time. And I'm getting better as an actor all the time. Come and work with Lord Strange's Men at the Rose theatre on Bankside. You can write for us.'

So we both went to the Rose. John Heminges came with us, and Augustine Phillips – he was a good actor, too.

We worked harder than ever at the Rose. Plays were always in the afternoon, because of the daylight. We had rehearsals in the morning, and by lunch-time people were already coming across the river to get their places for the play. And more and more people came. By 1592 London was hearing the name William Shakespeare again and again.

5
The plague years

Will wrote his play *Richard III* for Richard Burbage, and it was a great success. Richard the Third was a wicked king – a murderer – but he was wonderful on the stage, with Burbage's great voice and fine acting. Soon all London was saying King Richard's famous words when his horse is killed in war:

A horse! a horse! my kingdom for a horse!

All kinds of people came to see plays and Will was making a lot of new friends. One day, after the play, he was talking to a young man outside the Rose. He was a very beautiful young man, a bit like a girl, perhaps – but still very good-looking. Later, I asked Will who he was.

The Earl of Southampton
'He loves poetry and plays.'

'The Earl of Southampton,' Will said. 'He's only eighteen, but he loves poetry and plays.'

'Isn't he a friend of the Earl of Essex?' I asked. Everybody knew the Earl of Essex. He was young and good-looking – and some people said that Queen Elizabeth was in love with him.

I don't know about that. The Queen was fifty-nine years old, and a very, very clever woman. But it was true that she liked to have good-looking young men around her, and the Earl of Essex was her favourite. Then. It all changed later, of course.

'Yes, he is,' said Will. 'But I think Essex is a dangerous man. Henry needs better friends than him.'

'Henry, eh?' I said, surprised. 'My word! Do you really call him Henry? Not Lord Southampton?'

'Only when other people aren't there.' Will laughed. 'I'm still just an actor from Stratford, Toby. Not very important. Let's go and have a drink at the Boar's Head on our way home.'

Will was always like that. Quiet, never shouting about himself to the world.

In the Boar's Head we met some friends and started talking. The talk was all about the plague, which was coming back again into London.

'Have you heard the latest news?' said one man. 'They say that more than thirty people are dying every week now.'

'And the City Council,' said another man, 'wants to close all the theatres. They always do that when the plague comes to London. There'll be no work for any of us actors.'

'But the players can go on tour, surely?' said Will.

'Yes,' said the first man. 'But it's a hard life. A different town, a different inn, a different play, every night. I think I'll stay in London.'

The plague is terrible in any place, but it was worst in London. In those narrow streets, with houses so close together, and the dirty water running down the middle of the street, there was no escape. When the plague came, it ran like fire through the town. If someone in a house got the plague,

Lord, haue mercy
on London.
I follow.
We fly.
Wee dye.
Keepe out.

The plague is terrible in any place, but it was worst in London.

then the doors were shut and locked, and a big red cross was put on the door. Nobody could leave the house. You had to stay inside and fight – or die. If you were rich, you left London as fast as you could.

In September 1592 the City Council closed the theatres.

'Are we going on tour, Will?' I said to him one day. 'Or back to Stratford? We can't stay in London.'

'You go back to Stratford, Toby,' he said slowly. 'I'm going to Lord Southampton's home in Hampshire for a while. He's asked me to go and stay with him. I can do some writing there, read his books, meet a few people.'

I looked at him. 'There's a woman in this somewhere, isn't there? You've had a strange look in your eyes for weeks.'

Will laughed, but didn't answer my question.

The theatres in London didn't open again until June 1594. Will often visited Lord Southampton, but sometimes we went on tour with the company, or spent time at home in Stratford. Will began to spend more time in Stratford, because it was quiet there, and he could do his writing. I never heard what Anne thought about it all.

During those years Will wrote a lot of poetry. He wrote his beautiful long poem, *Venus and Adonis*, for his friend Lord Southampton, and he wrote many of his famous short poems, the Sonnets. But they didn't go in a book; they were only for his friends to read.

One day, when we were back in London, I was reading some of his latest sonnets. Will was out somewhere, and I was at home in our lodgings in Bishopsgate. A lot of the poems were about a woman, a terrible, black-haired, black-eyed woman. She was cold and cruel, then she was true and loving, and then she was cruel again.

For I have sworn thee fair, and thought thee bright,
Who art as black as hell, as dark as night.

Was Will writing about himself here? I asked myself. And who was this woman, this Dark Lady?

I always like to know what's going on, so I listened, and watched, and looked at all his women friends.

Then one day I saw her. I was coming in the door at our lodgings, and she was coming downstairs. She had black hair and great stormy black eyes, and there was gold at her ears and round her neck. I stood back and she went past me like a ship sailing into war. She looked wild, and angry, and very, very beautiful.

'Whew!' I said to myself. 'If that's Will's Dark Lady, he'll never have a quiet, easy life!'

The woman looked Italian, so I went and asked John Florio about her. Florio was Lord Southampton's Italian teacher. We saw a lot of him in those days.

I described the woman, and he knew her at once.

'Emilia,' he said. 'Emilia Bassano. Now Emilia Lanier, wife to Alphonso Lanier. Before that, she lived with the old Lord Chamberlain. She was not his wife, you understand. But why do you want to know, my friend?'

'If she's a married lady, she doesn't have a lover now, then?'

Florio laughed loudly. 'Lovers! You don't know Emilia Lanier! She's a bad woman, my friend, a bad woman.' Now he spoke very quietly. 'For a time she was the friend of Lord Southampton. But not now. That is all finished.'

I didn't ask him about Will. Perhaps Emilia Lanier was Will's Dark Lady, or perhaps Will was just trying to help his friend Lord Southampton. Nobody will ever know now.

6
Death in the family

After the plague years, we were busy all the time. There were new companies of players and Will now belonged to the Lord Chamberlain's Men. The Lord Chamberlain was a very important man, close to the Queen, and we often put on plays for the Queen's court, and in the houses of the great lords of England. We had some very good actors. There was Will, and Richard Burbage, of course, and John Heminges. And there was Augustine Phillips, Henry Condell, and Thomas Pope. There were other actors, too, but those six were the real company. They worked together for more than twenty years. And made a lot of money, too.

I did the costumes and properties for the Chamberlain's. John Heminges said I was the best properties man in the city.

Will was special – because he wrote the plays. And what plays they were! He never wrote the same play twice, like some writers. He was always trying something new, something different. And he wrote fast, too.

John Heminges could never understand that. 'How can you write so fast, Will?' he asked him. 'And you never make a mistake or change a word.'

Will didn't really understand it himself. 'It's all in my head,' he said. 'I think about it, and then it just comes out on paper.'

He wrote a play about love in 1595. Young love. It was *Romeo and Juliet*. It was a very sad play, because the young lovers die at the end. But the playgoers loved it. They wanted to see it again and again.

Will played the part of old Capulet, Juliet's father. One of the boy actors played the part of Juliet. There were no women actors, so boys played all the women's parts. Of course, Will never put real love-making on stage. He did it all with words – clever, beautiful words, and you forgot that the women and girls were really boys in dresses. Some of the boy actors were very good, and went on to play men's parts when they were older.

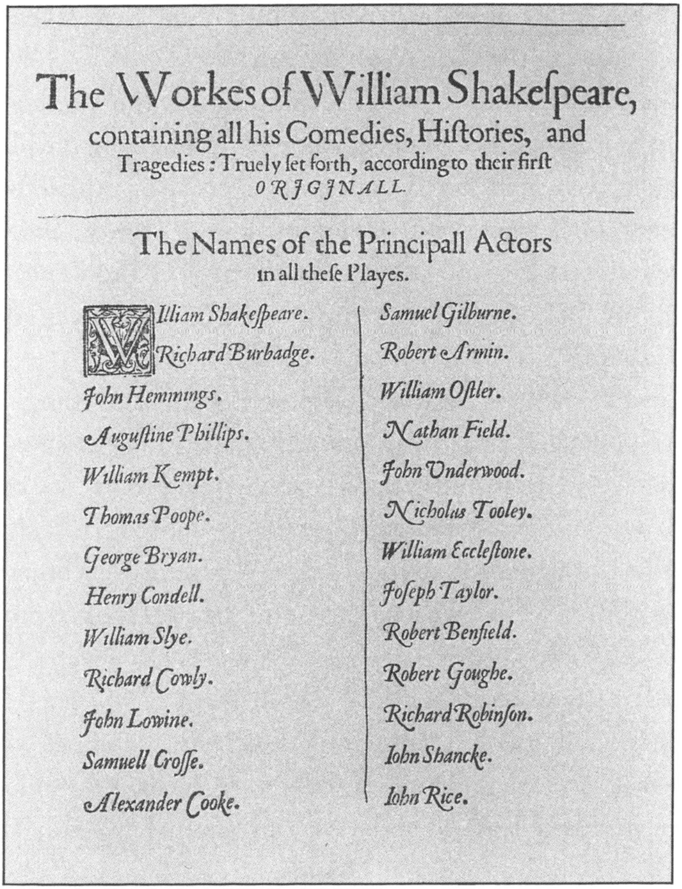

The Workes of William Shakeſpeare, containing all his Comedies, Hiſtories, and Tragedies: Truely ſet forth, according to their firſt ORIGINALL.

The Names of the Principall Actors in all theſe Playes.

William Shakeſpeare.	*Samuel Gilburne.*
Richard Burbadge.	*Robert Armin.*
John Hemmings.	*William Oſtler.*
Auguſtine Phillips.	*Nathan Field.*
William Kempt.	*John Underwood.*
Thomas Poope.	*Nicholas Tooley.*
George Bryan.	*William Eccleſtone.*
Henry Condell.	*Joſeph Taylor.*
William Slye.	*Robert Benfield.*
Richard Cowly.	*Robert Goughe.*
John Lowine.	*Richard Robinſon.*
Samuell Croſſe.	*Iohn Shancke.*
Alexander Cooke.	*Iohn Rice.*

We had some very good actors.

We played *Romeo and Juliet* at Richmond Palace that year. We always played before the Queen at Christmas. She liked to see the new plays, and she paid us £10 a play. We often had to work through the night to get the stage ready in time, but it was exciting to be in one of the Queen's palaces at Christmas. There was a lot of singing and dancing, and eating and drinking. Some years Christmas began in November and didn't finish until February or March.

The year 1596 began well, but that summer the weather was really bad. Cold. Wet. It never stopped raining, and the plague began to come back into London. We were in Stratford for the summer, but I went down to Hampshire for a few weeks to do some business for Will about some sheep. Will didn't need me at home, because he was busy writing his new play, *A Midsummer Night's Dream*.

I came back to Stratford one wet August evening. The house in Henley Street was strangely quiet, and I went round the back and up to Will's room – his writing room, we called it. He was just sitting there . . . not doing anything, just sitting.

'What's the matter, Will?' I said. 'Where *is* everybody?'

'At church.' His face was grey, and his eyes looked empty, dead.

'What's happened?' I asked. 'What is it?'

He looked at me. 'Hamnet . . .' he began. 'Hamnet was ill last week, and . . . and he died, yesterday. He was only eleven, Toby, and he's dead. My boy. My only son. He's dead, Toby. Dead.' He put his face in his hands.

What can you say to a man when something like that happens to him? I sat down next to him and put my hand on his arm. We sat together, silently. I knew that Will loved that boy of his – red-haired, bright as a new penny, full of life. Just like his father.

After a while I said, 'You'll have other sons.'

'Anne's forty already.' Will's voice was tired. 'She's had no children since the twins.'

'Well, now, you've got two fine girls in Susanna and Judith. They'll marry before long, and then you'll have more grandsons than you can count. You'll see. There'll be boys running up and down stairs, shouting for their Granddad Will!'

He smiled sadly, but his eyes were not so empty now. Pleased, I went on quickly:

'And there are all your brothers – Gilbert, Richard, Edmund. They'll have sons too. The Shakespeare family will never die out. Think of the family, Will, the family!'

And he did. He was already a famous poet and playwright, but he was a family man, too. The next year, 1597, he bought a new house for his family. It was a big, grand house, called New Place, right in the middle of Stratford. It cost £60 – a lot

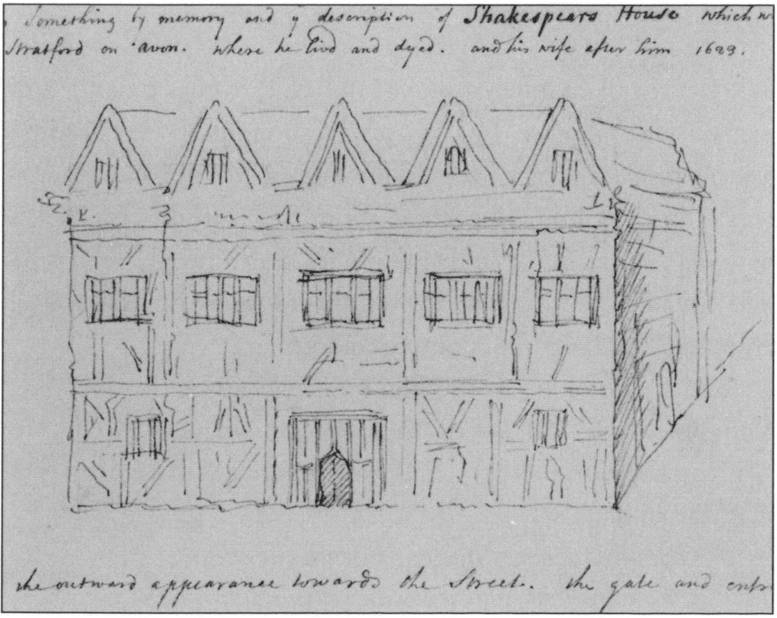

It was a big, grand house, called New Place.

of money – and the townspeople began to say 'Mr Shakespeare', not 'Young Will the actor' or 'John Shakespeare's boy'. They were happy to do business with him, and to borrow money from him.

Anne was very pleased with the new house. The wife of Mr Shakespeare of New Place was an important person in Stratford. But she still didn't like Will's work.

'Actors are wild, dangerous people,' she often said to him. 'I'm not interested in plays or the theatre, and I don't want to know anything about your work.'

But she liked the money, and the new house, and the new dresses – and the six fields of apple trees and the big farm north of Stratford that came a few years later.

Will never talked much about Hamnet. Life goes on and Will was busier than ever. But I know he thought about his son a lot; his grief was very deep inside him. A year or two later, I was talking to John Heminges about the costumes for Will's new play, *King John*. John Heminges was a family man – he had fourteen children in the end. The noise in his house! Shouting and laughing, coming and going . . .

John was looking at the playbook. 'You see this bit here, Toby,' he said. 'Will's writing about his son, isn't he?'

I read the words slowly, and remembered Will's empty eyes that day in August.

Grief fills the room up of my absent child,
Lies in his bed, walks up and down with me,
Puts on his pretty looks, repeats his words . . .

Richard Burbage said once that Will's writing changed after Hamnet's death. Will still laughed at people in his plays, but he also felt sorry for them – sorry for all the world, good and bad, rich and poor, young and old. And his people were real. No one was all good, or all bad.

There was a man called Shylock in his play *The Merchant of Venice*. This Shylock was a money-lender and a cruel man – everyone hated him. But in the end, when Shylock lost everything, you had to feel sorry for him. He was just a sad old man.

Perhaps Richard was right. And if anyone understood Will, it was Richard Burbage.

7
Queens, Kings, and Princes

Every year we took more and more plays to court at Christmas. In 1598 one of Will's plays was *Henry IV*. A lot of the play was about the King's son and his friend, Sir John Falstaff. Sir John was old, fat, lazy, drank too much, talked too much, laughed too much. But you had to love him. He was a great favourite with the London playgoers, and there were a lot of Falstaff jokes going round at the time.

After the play, the Queen wanted to speak to Will.

'Why? What have we done wrong?' John Heminges said to me in a very quiet voice.

'We'll find out in a minute,' I said.

We all watched while Will walked over to the Queen's

chair. She was an old woman, she wore a red wig, and she had black teeth. But she was still a very great queen. And if the Queen was not pleased . . .

She had a good, strong voice – an actor's voice. We could hear her easily.

'Mr Shakespeare,' she began. Then she smiled, and suddenly

Queen Elizabeth I

you knew why all Englishmen loved the Queen. It was like the sun coming out on a spring morning.

'Mr Shakespeare, you are the best playwright in England. I enjoyed your play, and I thought that Sir John Falstaff was very funny. I have known many Englishmen like him. Will you write me another play? I would like to see Sir John in love.'

When Will came back to us, his eyes were bright, but he was already thinking about it.

'Don't talk to me,' he said. 'I've got a play to write.'

He wrote it in two weeks, and we took it down to Richmond Palace and played it before the Queen on February the 20th. She laughed and laughed at *The Merry Wives of Windsor*.

She didn't have much to laugh about in 1599. There was a lot of trouble in Ireland, and the Queen sent the Earl of Essex with 20,000 men to fight a war. Lord Southampton, Will's friend, went with him. All London came out on to the streets to watch when Essex and his men left for Ireland. Will wrote an exciting play about war that summer, and he put in a word or two about Ireland. That was *Henry V*, about a very famous English King who fought a war in France.

But Essex was not Henry the Fifth. He didn't know how to fight a war, and he ran away back to England later that year. The Queen never spoke to him again.

In September we opened the Globe theatre. It was a grand, new building near the Rose. Will, Richard Burbage, and the others paid for it themselves. It was the best playhouse in London, and soon the most famous. The other companies had good theatres and some good actors, but we had the famous

In September we opened the Globe theatre.

Richard Burbage – and the best plays.

We put on three new plays by Will in the next year, and some plays by other writers. One of the new playwrights was Ben Jonson. He was a clever man and he wrote clever plays, but people still liked Will's plays best. Ben couldn't understand it. He was always arguing with Will about how to write plays. He argued with everyone. He went to prison once because he killed a man in a fight. He was eight years younger than Will, but he and Will were very good friends.

Will's next play was *Hamlet, Prince of Denmark.* We all met one day in the Boar's Head to talk about it. There were six of us – me and Will, Richard Burbage, Henry Condell, John Heminges, and Augustine Phillips.

Will put his pile of papers on the table and sat down.

'Well,' he said. 'You've all read it. What do you think?'

'It's very good,' John Heminges began, 'but it's too long. It'll take about four hours in the theatre.'

'We don't have to use it all,' Will said. 'We can cut it down to three hours, perhaps two and a half.'

Henry Condell picked up one of the papers from the table. 'Look at this bit, when Ophelia is talking about Hamlet,' he said. 'Hamlet sounds like the Earl of Essex to me. Were you thinking of Essex when you wrote this?'

Will smiled. 'Perhaps,' he said. 'And perhaps not.'

'Richard will play Prince Hamlet, yes?' said Augustine.

'Of course!' Will said. 'I wrote the part for him. He's our star actor. I'll play the ghost of Hamlet's father.' He looked at me. 'Hamlet will wear black, Toby, and Ophelia will wear white.'

Henry finished his beer. 'It's a good story, Will, with good parts for us all. But will the playgoers like it? It moves very slowly, and they like a play to be fast and exciting. Prince Hamlet knows that his uncle Claudius murdered the king his father. But he doesn't do anything about it for a long time. He just talks about it. And in the end nearly everybody dies, one way or another.'

Augustine didn't agree with that. 'You haven't understood the play, Henry. It *is* exciting, very exciting. The play is *inside* Hamlet himself. He wants to kill his uncle, but he can't. Murder is wrong. But he must kill him, because of his father. We can all understand how he feels.'

All this time Richard Burbage was silent. He was reading bits of the play again. Now he put down the paper in his hand and looked up. His eyes were bright, excited.

'Have any of you really listened to the language of this play? This is your best play yet, Will – the best of them all. Just listen

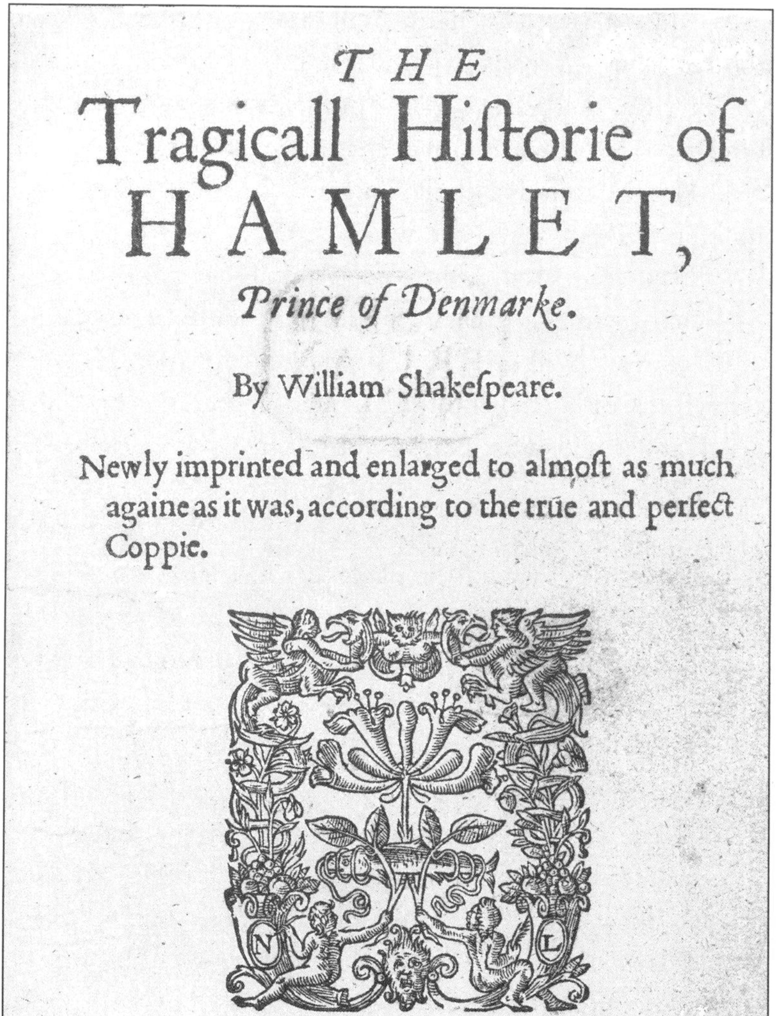

THE

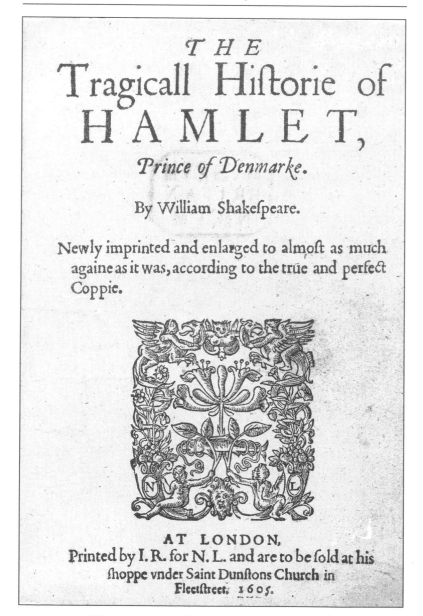

Tragicall Hiſtorie of

HAMLET,

Prince of Denmarke.

By William Shakeſpeare.

Newly imprinted and enlarged to almoſt as much againe as it was, according to the trûe and perfect Coppie.

AT LONDON,

Printed by I. R. for N. L. and are to be ſold at his ſhoppe vnder Saint Dunſtons Church in Fleetſtreet. 1605.

The title page of *Hamlet, Prince of Denmark*

to the language, the poetry!' He stood up, and his great voice filled the room.

To be, or not to be – that is the question . . .

We sat and listened, silently, while that wonderful voice brought the words to life. Will watched him, smiling. *He* knew that Richard, like him, was in love with words.

. . . To die, to sleep –
To sleep – perchance to dream. Ay, there's the rub.
For in that sleep of death what dreams may come
When we have shuffled off this mortal coil
*Must give us paus*e.

Richard Burbage was right, of course. The people loved the play, they loved Burbage as Hamlet, they cried for poor Ophelia's death, and they shouted for the murderer Claudius to die. I think it was Will's most famous play.

8
A Scottish King for England

Will's father died in September 1601. In his last years John Shakespeare was a happy man. His son was famous, and the Shakespeare family was important again in Stratford. But there weren't many children in the family. Will's sister Joan was married and had a little boy, but Will's brothers didn't have any children.

Susanna, Will's older daughter, was now eighteen, and Will said to her one day:

'We must find you a husband soon, Susanna.'

But Susanna shook her head. 'Oh, I don't want to be married, Father, thank you.'

We all smiled at that, because there was already a young man who was often a visitor at New Place. That was John Hall, a clever young doctor. Will liked him.

Back in London, the theatres were always full, and actors were now important people in the city. Will and I were now living in very fine lodgings in Silver Street, with the Mountjoy family. The Globe and the Lord Chamberlain's Men were doing very well, and the older actors in the company were making money, and buying houses and land. But some people still thought that actors were dangerous, wicked people.

Then Queen Elizabeth died, on the 24th of March 1603, at Richmond. I remember the day well. The theatres were closed – you can't have plays when a queen is dying – and we were all at Henry Condell's house. He and John Heminges lived very near our lodgings in Cripplegate.

We were all very worried. The new King of England was James the First. He was already King of Scotland, and he had a young wife, Queen Anne of Denmark, and three young children. But what was he like? Would he be a good king? And, most importantly, did he like plays?

'If King James doesn't like plays,' said Henry Condell, 'we're finished. There are already a lot of Puritans on the London City Council, and they'd love to close the theatres down.'

Henry always looked at the black side of everything.

'Well, he's written a lot of books himself,' said Will. 'Perhaps he'll be interested in plays, too. We'll just have to wait and see.'

We didn't have to wait long. On the 19th of May I was underneath the stage in the Globe. I was trying to mend a broken door in the floor of the stage. We used this door when a ghost came on or went off in a cloud of smoke. Suddenly, I heard feet running across the stage. I looked up through the

We used this door when a ghost came on in a cloud of smoke.

hole, and saw Will and John Heminges and Richard Burbage. They were all very excited.

'Listen to this, Toby,' said Will. He was holding a piece of paper in his hand. 'It's a letter from King James! From today, we are the King's Men! We're working for the King himself, and he wants to see all the plays.'

'We're going to have new red coats to wear when we go to court,' Richard said.

'And,' John said, 'he's going to pay us £20 for every play at court. What do you think about that, Toby?'

We were all laughing and smiling now. 'Well, John,' I said. 'If we're so rich, can I have a new door? I can't mend this one again – it's too old.'

That summer the plague came back. By July a thousand people were dying every week in London. One of them was the little son of Will's friend, Ben Jonson. By the end of the year there were 33,000 dead in England. The theatres closed, and the King's Men went on tour.

Will and I spent the summer at Stratford. When Christmas came, the King's Men put on a lot of plays at court. The King was at Hampton Court Palace that year, which was outside London, well away from the plague. I couldn't go because I fell off my horse one day and broke my leg. Stupid thing to do! I had to stay at home, but Will told me all about it when he came back.

'The new King and Queen like to enjoy themselves, Toby,' he said. 'They're a happy family. Prince Henry, who's nine, is

King James I of England

a very nice little boy, and his sister Elizabeth is beautiful. Little Prince Charles is only two.' He was silent for a minute. Perhaps he was thinking about Hamnet. Then he went on, 'Queen Anne likes plays very much. She likes music and dancing, too – she showed her legs in one dance!'

'My word!' I said. 'Things like that never happened at court in Queen Elizabeth's days.'

'We live in different times, Toby. A lot of things are going to change.'

But change only comes slowly. The King's Men went from one success to another. At the King's court at Christmas 1604, there were twenty-two plays, and eight of them were Will's. In 1605 there were thirteen plays at court – and ten of them were Will's.

We always did the plays at the Globe first, before we took them to court. Will was writing more slowly now, but during these years he wrote some of his best plays: *Othello*, *Macbeth*, and *King Lear*. That was a sad, dark play. When King Lear carried his dead daughter Cordelia on to the stage . . . Well, every man, woman, and child in the Globe was crying. It's true. Richard Burbage played Lear, of course. What an actor he was!

Richard Burbage
What an actor he was!

9
The Mermaid Tavern

During the next few years the plague was always with us. Some years it was bad, other years not so bad. When the theatres in London closed, we went on tour. Well, the King's Men did. Will and I were mostly at home in Stratford in the summers. Will was usually writing, and I did bits of business for him when I could.

Susanna married Dr John Hall in June, 1607, and Will's granddaughter Elizabeth was born in February the next year. We had a very cold winter that year. The river Thames in London froze right up to Westminster. People had parties and cooked sheep over fires on the ice.

Will's brother Edmund died that winter – he was only twenty-seven – and Will's mother died in September the next year.

Will was writing a different kind of play at this time. John Heminges said they were dark, cruel plays, and that Will was only looking at the black side of people. But that was the thing about Will. He was still changing, trying new kinds of poetry and stories in his plays all the time. And suddenly, there was a new kind of play, full of laughing and spring flowers and love: *The Winter's Tale*.

When we were in London, we often went in the evenings to the Mermaid Tavern in Cheapside. It was a very good inn, with good beer, and all the writers and poets in London went there.

We were there one evening in the winter of 1610, I think it

The river Thames froze right up to Westminster.

was. A lot of Will's friends were there – actors, writers. Ben Jonson was there, of course. He was a great drinker all his life. He was writing a lot of plays now and was doing very well. But he never had any money – Will always paid for the beer.

At first, the talk was all about King James and his court. We didn't like the King so much now – he was more interested in horses than in plays. Then Ben remembered something about *The Winter's Tale*. He knew, really, that Will's plays were the best, but he always liked to find mistakes if he could.

'Now, why did you put Bohemia by the sea, Will?' he said. 'Bohemia's in the middle of Europe! There's no sea for a hundred miles, you stupid man!'

'*Your* plays are very clever, Ben,' Richard Burbage said, 'but they smell of the schoolbook, don't they, Will?'

Will laughed. 'How many people are going to worry about that, Ben? What does it matter? They liked the play at court. The Queen said it was a very sweet play, and the King—'

'The King!' Ben said loudly. His face was red and angry. King James sometimes fell asleep during Ben's plays. 'The King,' he went on excitedly, 'is a very stupid man! I told him, I said it to his face: "Sir, you don't understand poetry!"'

John Heminges laughed. 'Oh my word!' he said. 'What a terrible man you are, Ben! I don't know how you've lived so long!'

Will laughed too, but he said, 'Ben, you must be careful. You don't want the King to be your enemy. Don't forget that he pays twice as much as Queen Elizabeth did – and sees twice as many plays.'

'Money?' shouted Ben. He loved to argue about anything. 'We're poets and actors, not businessmen! What does money matter?'

'It puts bread and meat in your stomach, and a coat on your back,' said Will, drinking his beer. 'And you're the first to shout if you haven't got any money.'

Ben banged his beer glass on the table. 'Now listen, Mr William Shakespeare of Stratford, with your fine big house and your expensive horses, you wrote in your play *King Lear* that money was—'

'Oh, do stop it, you two!' John Heminges said. He turned to talk to me, but a few minutes later Ben was arguing about another of Will's plays.

'And what about *Antony and Cleopatra*? What kind of writing is that? You never know which place you're in! One

Ben Jonson
He loved to argue about anything.

minute you're in Egypt, the next minute you're in Rome, then you're at sea on a ship, then back in Egypt again—'

Richard Burbage didn't like that. 'You're wrong again, Ben. It's only you who can't follow the play. You think Londoners are stupid, but they understand more than you do! And another thing . . .'

I decided to go home to bed. Ben's a fine man, but he does talk so much. He goes on and on. When I left, he was calling for more beer. I knew they would be there in the Mermaid for most of the night.

10
Back to Stratford

'You're losing your hair, Will,' I said to him one day.

'We're both getting old, Toby,' he said. 'There's no escape from it. Old and tired.'

'Don't talk like that,' I said. 'You're only forty-seven. There's still some life in you yet. And another twenty plays!'

'No,' he said slowly. 'No, I think the poetry is nearly finished. I'm getting tired, Toby. I need a rest. I think *The Tempest* is going to be my last play. I'm saying goodbye to the stage. Times are changing, and people want a different kind of play now. There are lots of new, younger writers, who know how to please the playgoer. I'm not modern any more.'

He never usually talked like this, and I didn't like it.

'There's only one Will Shakespeare,' I said, 'and he'll always be modern. Now, I must get on. I've got to go out and buy all the cloth for the new costumes in *The Tempest*. Why did you have to put it on an island? When the ship goes down, the actors all have to come on stage in wet clothes. It takes a day to dry the costumes, so that means two lots of clothes for everyone – wet and dry!'

That brought him back to life. 'Can't you read?' he said crossly. 'If you look at Gonzalo's words in Act 2, Toby, you'll see that it's a magic island – and their clothes stay dry all the time. So they'll only need one lot.'

I laughed, and then he laughed too.

But it was true, he *was* tired. I could see it, and others could see it too. But the company was always wanting new plays, and we had two theatres now. There was the Globe, and now we had the Blackfriars theatre. Plays in the Globe were in the open air and always had to be in daylight, but the Blackfriars was a building with a roof. We could put on plays in the evenings and in any weather. It also made more money, because every playgoer had a seat and paid a shilling for it. In the Globe they paid a penny to stand

In February 1612 Will's brother Gilbert died in London, and just a year later his brother Richard died in Stratford. That was in February, too. Will was the oldest brother, and he was the only one still alive. We spent most of our time in Stratford these days. Will didn't act in plays now. He went to rehearsals for his new plays, of course, but he was always happy to hurry home again.

We were riding back to Stratford in the spring of 1613 and stopped for the night at the Crown Inn in Oxford. Will was very friendly with the landlord John Davenant and his wife Jane. The next morning, when we left, their little son, William, came running out to say goodbye to his good friend

We were riding back to Stratford and stopped for the night in Oxford.

Mr Shakespeare. He was a bright boy, about seven years old, with much the same colour hair and eyes as Will. Will talked with him for a few minutes, then gave him a penny.

Later, when we were riding along the road, I said, 'The last time we were in Oxford, I heard some talk in the town. Someone said that *you* were the father of Jane Davenant's son.'

Will laughed. 'Well, well,' he said, 'people say that, do they? What *will* they say next?'

'Jane's a nice-looking woman.' I looked at him out of the corner of my eye. 'Isn't she?'

'Come on, Toby. You know that Jane is a good wife to John.' He was still smiling. 'You mustn't listen to stories like that.'

I never believed that story myself. But many years after Will died, William Davenant told a lot of people that he was Shakespeare's son. But how did he know? His mother wouldn't tell him!

Will was happy to get home, to see his daughters and John Hall, and little Elizabeth, who was just five then. He was happy to see Anne, I think. He never said much to her, nor she to him. But after more than thirty years together, you've already said everything, haven't you?

I think Judith was Will's favourite daughter. Susanna was brighter and cleverer, but Judith was Hamnet's twin, and Will still remembered his son. He wanted a son, or a grandson, so much. Judith was twenty-eight now, and still no husband. But Will told her not to hurry. She must find the right man first.

Will worked hard all his life, and I think it was all for his family. I remember some lines from his play *The Tempest*, when Prospero is talking to his daughter Miranda.

I have done nothing but in care of thee,
Of thee, my dear one, thee my daughter . . .

11
The last years

Will did write another play, of course. That was *Henry VIII* and he wrote it because the King's daughter, Princess Elizabeth, was getting married. The King's Men had to have a new play for a special day like that.

We were in London for rehearsals at the Globe, and the actors put on the new play for the first time on the 29th of June, 1613. I remember the date well.

It happened soon after the play began. Richard Burbage was on stage and he suddenly looked up and stopped in the middle of a word.

'Fire!' he shouted. 'The theatre's on fire!'

Wooden buildings burn fast, and Henry Condell shouted, 'Everybody out! Quickly!'

The crowd of playgoers began to hurry to the doors, and I ran round to open them. We could all see the smoke now, and John Heminges shouted to Will, 'The playbooks! We must get the playbooks out!'

Everybody got out and no one was hurt. One man's coat caught fire and his friend put the fire out with a bottle of beer.

'The theatre's on fire!'

But the Globe burnt right down to the ground in an hour. Poor old John Heminges just stood there and cried.

But you can't kill a theatre that easily. A year later there was a new Globe in the same place. Bigger and better than the old one. People said it was the finest playhouse in England.

We didn't often go to London in those last years. Will was happy at home in Stratford with his family. He had time for his garden, time to talk to his Stratford friends, time to play with his granddaughter Elizabeth. He read his plays again, and he and I talked and laughed about the old days.

Judith got married at last in February 1616. She was thirty-one then, and married a man called Thomas Quiney, who was twenty-six. Will wasn't too happy about it.

'Judith loves him very much,' he said quietly to me. 'But I'm not sure about him. I think she's making a mistake.'

He was right, of course. Will was usually right about people. Thomas Quiney was lazy, drank too much, and went with other women.

But Will didn't live to find that out. In March he went to London for a party at the Mermaid Tavern. Ben Jonson was now the playwright for the court of King James. The King was paying him some money every year, and Ben wanted to give a party for his friends.

It was a good party at the Mermaid, I heard.

It was a good party, I heard. But Will caught a fever and then rode home through the cold spring rain. When he got back to New Place, he was not a well man.

He died on the 23rd of April, in the year 1616.

They put his body in Holy Trinity Church, down by the river Avon. It was a bright, windy day, I remember. Ben Jonson came down from London, and cried in the church. He was a wild man, was Ben, always fighting and arguing about plays and poetry. But he loved his friend. He came up to me outside the church.

'Toby,' he said. 'Will was a good, true man, and I loved him. We'll never see another poet like him in England.'

12
England will remember

Well, all that was thirty-three years ago. I'm an old man, and everyone is dying around me. Anne Shakespeare died in 1623, and John Hall went about twelve years later, fighting the plague. Susanna's still alive, and Judith. She had three sons, but they all died. So there's no boy in the family to keep poor Will's name alive. Susanna's girl Elizabeth has had no children, and she's forty-one already . . . Susanna still comes to visit me sometimes, and we talk about the old days.

We live in sad times now; the Puritans cut King Charles's

He was the finest poet that ever wrote in the English language.

head off last January. But one day we'll have a king again. Then there'll be singing and dancing and plays.

You'll see. Oh yes. People won't forget William Shakespeare. In 400 years' time, the theatres will still be full. People will still laugh, and cry, over his plays. He was the finest poet that ever wrote in the English language. I think he knew that himself. There's some lines in one of his sonnets, I remember . . .

Not marble, nor the gilded monuments
Of princes shall outlive this powerful rhyme . . .

QUOTATIONS IN THE STORY

Shakespeare's poetry has many meanings. Here are some possible meanings of the quotations which are given in the story.

A horse! a horse! my kingdom for a horse! *Richard III, Act 4, iv*

I need a horse! I will give my kingdom for a horse!

For I have sworn thee fair, and thought thee bright,
Who art as black as hell, as dark as night. *Sonnets, 147*

I thought you were beautiful, loving and true, but really you are cold and cruel, and dangerous to know.

Grief fills the room up of my absent child,
Lies in his bed, walks up and down with me,
Puts on his pretty looks, repeats his words . . . *King John, Act 3, iv*

Sadness has taken the place of my child. He has gone, but I still see him – lying in his bed, walking next to me; I see his sweet face, I hear his words . . .

To be, or not to be – that is the question . . .
. . . To die, to sleep –
To sleep – perchance to dream. Ay, there's the rub,
For in that sleep of death what dreams may come
When we have shuffled off this mortal coil
Must give us pause. *Hamlet, Act 3, i*

To live, or to die – that is the question . . . If death is like sleep, perhaps we will dream. Yes, that's the problem. Because we don't know what kind of dreams we will have when we have died, and that makes us afraid.

I have done nothing but in care of thee,
Of thee, my dear one, thee my daughter . . . *The Tempest, Act 1, ii*

Everything I have done has been to take care of you, my dear daughter . . .

Not marble, nor the gilded monuments
Of princes shall outlive this powerful rhyme . . . *Sonnets, 55*

This poetry will live longer than stone or the golden buildings of princes . . .

GLOSSARY

actor a person who acts in plays in a theatre
argue to say that something is wrong or not true when you don't agree with it
beer a strong, brown-coloured drink
believe to think that something is right or true
company (of players) a group of actors who work together
costume the special clothes that an actor wears
council a group of people who govern a town or city
court the place where the king or queen and their followers meet
cruel very, very unkind
Earl a man from an important family
fever an illness when the body gets very hot
freeze (past tense **froze**) to get very cold (e.g. when water changes to ice)
ghost a dead person that living people think they can see
glove a cover for the hand
grief great sadness
ice water that is hard because it is very cold
inn a house where people can buy food and drink, and sometimes stay the night
joke something that somebody says to make other people laugh
lady a woman
landlord a man who has an inn
Latin the language of ancient Rome (now the capital of Italy)
lodgings rooms in a family house where you pay to live
lord a man from an important family
magic when strange and wonderful things happen

palace a large and beautiful house, usually for a king or queen
part a person in a play, e.g. *He played the part of Romeo*
plague an illness in Shakespeare's time which killed people very quickly
play *(v)* to act a part in a play in the theatre
playwright a person who writes plays
poetry pieces of writing in very beautiful language
poet a person who writes poetry
properties (in a theatre) the things which are needed on stage for a play, e.g. chairs, tables, boxes, bags, plates, a tree
Puritans some people in the Church of England in Shakespeare's time, who thought it was wicked for people to enjoy themselves
rehearsal when actors practise a play before they act in front of other people
sad unhappy
serious not laughing or playing or joking
shilling a coin in old English money (about 5p today)
sonnet a poem of fourteen lines
stage the part of a theatre where actors stand and move
success something that is popular and pleases people
tour (to go on tour) to travel round the country and put on a play in different places
twins two children born from the same mother at the same time
uncle the brother of your mother or father
war fighting between countries
wicked very bad or wrong
wig hair which is not real
worried feeling that something is wrong or will be wrong

ACTIVITIES

Before Reading

1 Read the back cover of the book, and the story introduction on the first page. What do you know now about this story? Tick one box for each sentence.

	YES	NO
1 William Shakespeare was born in London.	☐	☐
2 He was an actor and a playwright.	☐	☐
3 He wrote nearly forty plays.	☐	☐
4 He had five children.	☐	☐
5 He wrote the play *Romeo and Juliet*.	☐	☐
6 Toby was a real person.	☐	☐

2 What will you find out about Shakespeare from this story? Can you guess? Tick one box for each sentence.

	YES	NO
1 In London he is a very famous actor.	☐	☐
2 The Queen of England likes his plays.	☐	☐
3 He works hard all his life.	☐	☐
4 He gets into trouble and goes to prison.	☐	☐
5 He leaves his wife Anne and marries again.	☐	☐
6 He makes money and buys houses and land.	☐	☐
7 He dies in Stratford-upon-Avon.	☐	☐
8 He has grandsons who carry on his name.	☐	☐

ACTIVITIES

While Reading

Read Chapters 1 to 4. Choose the best question-word for these questions, and then answer them.

How / What / Which / Why

1 . . . play was acted for the Queen on 6th January 1601?
2 . . . did Will have to do at school?
3 . . . was John Shakespeare's business?
4 . . . old was Will when he got married?
5 . . . was Anne's name before she married Will?
6 . . . company of players came to Stratford in June 1587?
7 . . . did Will decide to go to London?
8 . . . many people lived in the City of London then?
9 . . . was the theatre in Shoreditch called?
10 . . . did Toby decide not to be an actor?
11 . . . was Will like as an actor?
12 . . . theatre was Richard Burbage acting in then?

Before you read Chapter 5 (*The Plague Years*), can you guess what happens? Choose words for each sentence.

1 *A few / Thousands of* people die from the plague.
2 During the plague the London theatres *close / stay open.*
3 Will spends *all / some* of his time back in Stratford.
4 Will writes some *poems / plays* about *a child / a woman.*

Read Chapters 5 and 6, and answer these questions.

1 Who was Will's fine new friend?
2 If you were rich, what did you do during the plague?
3 What did Will do in Hampshire?
4 Why did Toby watch all Will's women friends?
5 Which company of players did Will now belong to?
6 What work did Toby do in this company?
7 Who played the women's parts on stage?
8 What happened in the Queen's palaces at Christmas?
9 What happened in August 1596?
10 Why did people begin to call Will 'Mr Shakespeare'?
11 What were the things that made Anne happy?
12 How did Will's writing change after Hamnet's death?

Read Chapters 7 to 9, and answer these questions.

Who

1 . . . did the Queen send to fight a war in Ireland?
2 . . . paid for the new Globe theatre?
3 . . . was the star actor in the Lord Chamberlain's Men?
4 . . . played the ghost of Hamlet's father on stage?
5 . . . died at Richmond in March 1603?
6 . . . wanted to close the theatres down?
7 . . . was born in Stratford in February 1608?
8 . . . went to the Mermaid Tavern in Cheapside?
9 . . . wrote plays that 'smelled of the schoolbook'?
10 . . . sometimes fell asleep during Ben Jonson's plays?

In Chapters 7 to 9, who said this? And who or what were they talking about?

1 'I would like to see Sir John in love.'
2 'We can cut it down to three hours . . .'
3 'We must find you a husband soon . . .'
4 'From today, we are the King's Men!'
5 'Bohemia's in the middle of Europe!'

Before you read the last chapters, can you guess the answers to these questions?

1 What does Shakespeare write in his last years?
  a) Nothing. b) Two more plays. c) Ten more plays.
2 How does Shakespeare die?
  a) In a fight. b) From the plague. c) From a fever.

Read Chapters 10 to 12. Can you find and correct the mistakes in this passage?

In Shakespeare's poem *The Tempest*, he said goodbye to the world, and it was his last play. His two older sisters died, and he spent less time in Stratford with his family. In June 1613 the Rose burnt down, and many people were hurt. Will went to a party at the Boar's Head, caught the plague, and died in London in June, 1636. His body lies in a palace by the river Thames. He had three grandsons to carry on his name, but nobody has remembered the name Shakespeare.

ACTIVITIES

After Reading

1 **Match the sentences with the people below. Then choose the best ending for each sentence and complete it with pronouns (*he, she, they, her, their, who*).**

Anne Shakespeare / Richard Burbage / Susanna / Judith / Hamnet / Ben Jonson / Queen Elizabeth / The Dark Lady

1 _____ liked to see all the new plays, . . .
2 _____ was Judith's twin and Will's only son, . . .
3 _____ was a woman in Shakespeare's sonnets, . . .
4 _____ did not like plays or the theatre, . . .
5 _____ married a man called Thomas Quiney, . . .
6 _____ was a playwright and a good friend of Will's, . . .
7 _____ was a famous actor in Will's company, . . .
8 _____'s husband was a doctor called John Hall, . . .

9 but nobody knows who _____ was in real life.
10 _____ played many of the big parts in Will's plays.
11 so the company acted in _____ palaces at Christmas.
12 but _____ three sons all died when _____ were young.
13 and _____ daughter Elizabeth was eight when Will died.
14 but _____ died when _____ was eleven years old.
15 _____ loved arguing about plays and poetry.
16 because _____ thought actors were wicked people.

2 **Two playgoers, Nathan and Samuel, are arguing about plays. Put their conversation in the right order, and write in the speakers' names. Samuel speaks first (number 3).**

1 _____ 'Did you like Will's *Romeo and Juliet* then? You remember that play? There were lovers in that.'

2 _____ 'Yes, I did, but *Hamlet* was so sad. Everybody dies at the end. I like plays with jokes, and lovers.'

3 _____ 'Have you seen *King Lear*, Nathan? It's Will Shakespeare's new play at the Globe.'

4 _____ 'But it wasn't funny, was it? Romeo and Juliet kill themselves! No, I like a happy ending myself.'

5 _____ 'Yes, he is. Did you see him in *Hamlet*?'

6 _____ 'No, I haven't. Is it any good? Who's in it?'

7 _____ 'You mean like the happy ending in *Twelfth Night* – that play with Sir Toby Belch in it.'

8 _____ 'Dead daughter? Oh, I don't think I want to see that. I hope they do *The Merry Wives of Windsor* again. I'd like to see that again – I loved it.'

9 _____ 'Richard Burbage. He plays the King.'

10 _____ 'Yes, Sir Toby was great! It was very funny, that play. Is there anything to laugh at in this new play?'

11 _____ 'Well, Nathan, there are no merry wives in *King Lear*. But it's a great play. You must see it!'

12 _____ 'Oh, I like Burbage. He's a very good actor.'

13 _____ 'No, you won't laugh, you'll cry. When King Lear carries his dead daughter on to the stage—'

3 Here are 16 of Shakespeare's plays from the story, but the titles are mixed up. Can you put the right parts together?

Macbeth the Third	Henry and Cleopatra
John the Fourth	The Night
Lear the Fifth	The Merry Wives of Venice
Romeo	A Midsummer Night's Tale
Henry	The Merchant of Denmark
King Othello	Twelfth Tempest
King Antony	The Winter's Dream
Richard and Juliet	Hamlet, Prince of Windsor

4 There are 17 words from the story (6 of them are plural words) hidden in this word search. Find the words (they go from left to right, and from top to bottom), and draw lines through them.

P	T	S	O	N	N	E	T	O	P	A	R	T	S
L	B	R	E	O	W	I	C	K	E	D	R	M	N
A	O	E	P	L	A	Y	G	O	E	R	S	U	T
Y	T	H	T	A	O	J	O	K	E	S	B	R	E
W	T	E	H	F	H	F	U	N	N	Y	A	D	C
R	T	A	E	R	P	O	E	T	R	Y	I	E	L
I	S	R	A	A	T	K	I	N	G	S	H	R	E
G	E	S	T	I	L	O	V	E	R	S	Q	E	V
H	U	A	R	D	E	S	A	C	T	O	R	R	E
T	T	L	E	I	S	T	A	G	E	O	N	S	R

Which 7 words are about theatres and plays?

5 **Now use 14 of the words from the word search to complete this passage about Shakespeare.**

Shakespeare was a _____ who also worked in the _____. He was an _____ himself, playing small _____ in his own plays, and he knew what the London _____ liked. He gave them _____ to make them laugh, and ghosts to make them _____. He gave them _____ and queens, thieves and _____, soldiers and _____ – real people, who were _____ and cruel, _____ and stupid, _____ and sad. Shakespeare died when he was only 52, but his plays and his _____ live on.

6 **Look at the word search again, and write down all the letters without a line through them. Begin with the first line, and go across each line to the end. You will have 30 letters, which will make a sentence of 10 words.**

1 What is the sentence, and where does it come from?
2 Who first said it on the stage, and in which theatre?
3 What do you think the person was thinking about?

7 **What kind of stories in plays, films, or books do *you* like? Choose some of these sentences and complete them.**

1 I like stories *about* / *with* _________.
2 *Happy* / *sad* endings are best, because _________.
3 I *like* / *don't like* stories which _________.
4 I like stories in *plays* / *films* / *books* because _________.

ABOUT SHAKESPEARE TODAY

Nearly 400 years after William Shakespeare's death, people are still enjoying his plays and his poetry. Year after year there are new books about his life and his works; the Royal Shakespeare Company performs the plays in theatres in Stratford, London, and around the country; and there are new versions on the radio, on television, and on film.

In 1997 the new Globe Theatre, which was the idea of Sam Wanamaker, an American actor and director, was opened in

Henry V, *performed by the Globe Theatre Company in 1997, at the new Globe Theatre in Southwark, London*

Southwark, London, by Queen Elizabeth II. The new Globe, like Shakespeare's Globe, is a round building, open to the sky, and is built of English oak. It stands only 200 metres from where Shakespeare's Globe once stood. Performances are in daylight, and some of the audience ('the groundlings') stand in the yard, just as they did 400 years ago.

Shakespeare's plays are performed all over the world, and in many different ways. There are Italian operas and American musicals – *West Side Story* was based on *Romeo and Juliet*. There are many famous films, including a Russian *Hamlet* and a Japanese *King Lear*. A film in 1999, called *Shakespeare in Love*, gave us a picture of Shakespeare as a young man in London, writing *Romeo and Juliet*, falling in love, and living life to the full. The film was a great success. William Shakespeare has not been forgotten.

ABOUT THE AUTHOR

Jennifer Bassett has worked in English Language Teaching since 1972. She has been a teacher, teacher trainer, editor, and materials writer, and has taught in England, Greece, Spain, and Portugal. She is the current Series Editor of the Oxford Bookworms Library, and has written several other stories for the series, including *One-Way Ticket* and *The Phantom of the Opera* (both at Stage 1). She lives and works in Devonshire, in the south-west of England.

For this story about William Shakespeare, she used information from his plays and poems, and from some of the hundreds of books about him. She has seen nearly all the plays in the theatre or on film – some of them six or seven times – and she loves going to the new Globe Theatre in London.

OXFORD BOOKWORMS LIBRARY

Classics • Crime & Mystery • Factfiles • Fantasy & Horror
Human Interest • Playscripts • Thriller & Adventure
True Stories • World Stories

The OXFORD BOOKWORMS LIBRARY provides enjoyable reading in English, with a wide range of classic and modern fiction, non-fiction, and plays. It includes original and adapted texts in seven carefully graded language stages, which take learners from beginner to advanced level. An overview is given on the next pages.

All Stage 1 titles are available as audio recordings, as well as over eighty other titles from Starter to Stage 6. All Starters and many titles at Stages 1 to 4 are specially recommended for younger learners. Every Bookworm is illustrated, and Starters and Factfiles have full-colour illustrations.

The OXFORD BOOKWORMS LIBRARY also offers extensive support. Each book contains an introduction to the story, notes about the author, a glossary, and activities. Additional resources include tests and worksheets, and answers for these and for the activities in the books. There is advice on running a class library, using audio recordings, and the many ways of using Oxford Bookworms in reading programmes. Resource materials are available on the website <www.oup.com/elt/gradedreaders>.

The *Oxford Bookworms Collection* is a series for advanced learners. It consists of volumes of short stories by well-known authors, both classic and modern. Texts are not abridged or adapted in any way, but carefully selected to be accessible to the advanced student.

You can find details and a full list of titles in the *Oxford Bookworms Library Catalogue* and *Oxford English Language Teaching Catalogues*, and on the website <www.oup.com/elt/gradedreaders>.

THE OXFORD BOOKWORMS LIBRARY GRADING AND SAMPLE EXTRACTS

STARTER • 250 HEADWORDS

present simple – present continuous – imperative – *can/cannot, must* – *going to* (future) – simple gerunds …

Her phone is ringing – but where is it?

Sally gets out of bed and looks in her bag. No phone. She looks under the bed. No phone. Then she looks behind the door. There is her phone. Sally picks up her phone and answers it. ***Sally's Phone***

STAGE 1 • 400 HEADWORDS

… past simple – coordination with *and, but, or* – subordination with *before, after, when, because, so* …

I knew him in Persia. He was a famous builder and I worked with him there. For a time I was his friend, but not for long. When he came to Paris, I came after him – I wanted to watch him. He was a very clever, very dangerous man. ***The Phantom of the Opera***

STAGE 2 • 700 HEADWORDS

… present perfect – *will* (future) – *(don't) have to, must not, could* – comparison of adjectives – simple *if* clauses – past continuous – tag questions – *ask/tell* + infinitive …

While I was writing these words in my diary, I decided what to do. I must try to escape. I shall try to get down the wall outside. The window is high above the ground, but I have to try. I shall take some of the gold with me – if I escape, perhaps it will be helpful later. ***Dracula***

STAGE 3 • 1000 HEADWORDS

... *should, may* – present perfect continuous – *used to* – past perfect – causative – relative clauses – indirect statements ...

Of course, it was most important that no one should see Colin, Mary, or Dickon entering the secret garden. So Colin gave orders to the gardeners that they must all keep away from that part of the garden in future. ***The Secret Garden***

STAGE 4 • 1400 HEADWORDS

... past perfect continuous – passive (simple forms) – *would* conditional clauses – indirect questions – relatives with *where/when* – gerunds after prepositions/phrases ...

I was glad. Now Hyde could not show his face to the world again. If he did, every honest man in London would be proud to report him to the police. ***Dr Jekyll and Mr Hyde***

STAGE 5 • 1800 HEADWORDS

... future continuous – future perfect – passive (modals, continuous forms) – *would have* conditional clauses – modals + perfect infinitive ...

If he had spoken Estella's name, I would have hit him. I was so angry with him, and so depressed about my future, that I could not eat the breakfast. Instead I went straight to the old house. ***Great Expectations***

STAGE 6 • 2500 HEADWORDS

... passive (infinitives, gerunds) – advanced modal meanings – clauses of concession, condition

When I stepped up to the piano, I was confident. It was as if I knew that the prodigy side of me really did exist. And when I started to play, I was so caught up in how lovely I looked that I didn't worry how I would sound. ***The Joy Luck Club***